EXPLORERS

La Salle

Kristin Petrie

ABDO
Publishing Company

visit us at
www.abdopublishing.com

Published by ABDO Publishing Company, 4940 Viking Drive, Edina, Minnesota 55435.
Copyright © 2007 by Abdo Consulting Group, Inc. International copyrights reserved in all
countries. No part of this book may be reproduced in any form without written permission from
the publisher. The Checkerboard Library™ is a trademark and logo of ABDO Publishing
Company.

Printed in the United States.

Cover Photos: North Wind
Interior Photos: Corbis pp. 15, 17, 27; North Wind pp. 5, 7, 9, 11, 13, 19, 21, 25, 29

Series Coordinator: Heidi M. Dahmes
Editors: Rochelle Baltzer, Heidi M. Dahmes
Art Direction & Cover Design: Neil Klinepier
Interior Design & Maps: Dave Bullen

Library of Congress Cataloging-in-Publication Data

Petrie, Kristin, 1970-
  La Salle / Kristin Petrie.
    p. cm. -- (Explorers)
  Includes index.
  ISBN-10 1-59679-750-9
  ISBN-13 978-1-59679-750-5
  1. La Salle, Robert Cavelier, sieur de, 1643-1687--Juvenile literature. 2. Explorers--North
America--Biography--Juvenile literature. 3. Explorers--France--Biography--Juvenile literature.
4. Canada--Discovery and exploration--French--Juvenile literature. 5. Canada--History--To 1763
(New France)--Juvenile literature. 6. Mississippi River Valley--Discovery and exploration--
French--Juvenile literature. 7. Mississippi River Valley--History--To 1803--Juvenile literature.
I. Title. II. Series: Petrie, Kristin, 1970-   . Explorers.
F1030.5.P38 2006
977.01'092--dc22
  [B]
                                                                              2005017495

Contents

La Salle

France, the Mississippi River, and the **Louisiana Purchase** have one thing in common. They are all linked to a French explorer named René-Robert Cavelier. He is better known as Sieur de La Salle. La Salle dreamed of a large French empire in the New World.

In the late 1600s, La Salle was the first European to explore the length of the great Mississippi River. As a result of La Salle's determination, France claimed the entire Mississippi River **basin**. That's more than 800,000 square miles (2,072,000 sq km) of land!

In 1803, the United States bought this territory from France. This agreement is known as the Louisiana Purchase. It doubled the size of the United States and contributed to America's westward expansion.

La Salle's vision of a French empire in the New World was never realized. Still, his many explorations provided hope for France. Through both success and failure, La Salle became one of history's great explorers.

1271
Polo left for Asia

1295
Polo returned to Italy

1254
Marco Polo born

1275
Polo met Kublai Khan

During René-Robert Cavelier de La Salle's time, North America was a vast wilderness. The New World's mysteries drew La Salle to a life of exploration.

1460 or 1474
Juan Ponce de León born

1480
Ferdinand Magellan born

1324
Polo died

1475
Vasco Núñez de Balboa born

Early Years

René-Robert Cavelier was born on November 22, 1643, in Rouen, France. René-Robert's father, Jean Cavelier, was a successful merchant. His mother was Catherine Geest. René-Robert was the couple's second child.

The Cavelier family was wealthy. They lived on a farm in the Seine River valley. Their land was called "La Salle." At that time, parents honored a son by giving him a title that included the name of their estate. That is how René-Robert Cavelier became known as La Salle.

The Cavelier children grew up in a **strict** household. René-Robert's schooling started when he was very young. He was **tutored** at home. He learned how to read and write. He also received instruction in manners.

Growing up, René-Robert showed a special interest in books. He loved geography, history, and religion. And, he was gifted in mathematics. Jean and Catherine thought he would become a lawyer. However, René-Robert had other ideas.

1500
Balboa joined expedition to South America

1493
Ponce de León joined expedition to New World

1502
Ponce de León became governor of Higüey

Rouen is a port city along the Seine River, just northwest of Paris.

1508	1514
Ponce de León's first expedition	Ponce de León knighted by King Ferdinand II

1513
Ponce de León's second expedition, discovered Florida and the Gulf Stream; Balboa was the first European to sight the Pacific Ocean

The Jesuits

When he was 15, René-Robert entered a **Jesuit** school in Rouen. There, he heard tales of **missionaries** traveling to faraway places. They earned respect by bravely entering the wilderness of the New World to spread Christianity. René-Robert longed to see new lands.

At 16, René-Robert began studying to be a priest. The Jesuits demanded a strong education. So, he attended respected colleges in Rouen and later La Flèche. René-Robert studied subjects such as **astronomy** and navigation. The more he learned, the greater his urge to travel became.

When his studies were complete, René-Robert began teaching. However, he was restless. He wished to begin missionary work. René-Robert made several requests to be sent to the New World as a missionary. However, each request was denied. René-Robert became angry. So in 1665, he left the Jesuits.

1520
Magellan discovered the Strait of Magellan

1554
Walter Raleigh born

1519
Magellan led expedition to Spice Islands; Balboa died

1521
Ponce de León's third expedition, died in Cuba; Magellan died

Would You?

Would you enjoy being a missionary? Do you think it would be exciting to travel to foreign lands and learn new languages?

Travel and Work

On his own, La Salle found himself in a difficult situation. During his time with the **Jesuits**, La Salle had taken a vow of poverty. So when his father had passed away, he had not inherited any money or land. Now, La Salle had to figure out how to earn a living.

La Salle's older brother, Jean, was a **missionary** in New France. This was the area of French colonies in North America. La Salle also had cousins that had been living in New France for ten years. They had become successful in the trading business.

With these connections, La Salle decided to journey to New France. Travel was what he wanted most! If he could not get to foreign lands as a missionary, he would do it on his own. So in 1666, La Salle boarded a ship for New France.

1580
John Smith born

1585
Raleigh knighted by Queen Elizabeth I

1565
Henry Hudson born

1584–1589
Raleigh sponsored expeditions

Would You?

Would you jump on a ship if you had no money? Do you think La Salle had plans for what he would do in New France? What do you think he took with him?

New France

The late 1600s was a good time to set sail for the New World. Other explorers had been working hard to settle the land. And, the trading business was booming.

After several weeks on the choppy Atlantic Ocean, La Salle caught his first glimpse of the New World. His ship headed inland on the St. Lawrence River. At last, the ship reached the French settlement called Quebec.

In Quebec, La Salle quickly made plans to sail to Montreal. Montreal was on the border of French civilization. Wilderness surrounded this primitive town that **Sulpician** priests had bravely established.

In Montreal, the Sulpicians gave La Salle a large piece of land to settle. La Salle was not accustomed to hard work. But with the help of a team of laborers, a village took form. La Salle named his estate Saint Sulpice.

1595
Raleigh led first expedition

1588
Raleigh helped defeat the Spanish Armada

1606
Smith joined expedition to North America

La Salle spent the next three years farming and trading. Natives provided him with valuable furs. Despite his success, La Salle remained restless. He began wandering into the wilderness surrounding Saint Sulpice. The desire for adventure burned within him.

Natives provided La Salle with furs, which he exported to Europe.

Beautiful River

In 1668, La Salle's curiosity grew even stronger. Two Iroquois Native Americans arrived at Saint Sulpice. La Salle allowed them to make their winter camp on his land. During the cold months, La Salle learned the Iroquois **dialect**. He listened to the natives talk about a river to the southwest. They called it the Ohio, which means "beautiful river."

The natives said the Ohio flowed west into the sea. Back then, a large river flowing west could mean great things. Explorers had been searching for a waterway connecting the Atlantic and Pacific oceans. If the passage existed, it would make an ideal westward route to the **Far East**.

After thinking about this possibility, La Salle made a new goal. He talked excitedly about plans for an expedition down the Ohio River. During his planning, he also heard many stories about another river called the Mississippi. He was told that the great Mississippi River ran to a sea, too.

1607
Hudson's first expedition

1609
Hudson's third expedition

1608
Hudson's second expedition

The Ohio River flows southwest from Pittsburgh, Pennsylvania, to Cairo, Illinois.

La Salle thought one of these rivers might lead to the Pacific. He became even more excited and determined to go exploring. But first, he needed permission and money for an expedition.

1614
Smith led expedition to North America, charted and named New England

1610–1611
Hudson's last expedition, he died

1616
Raleigh's second expedition

Into Wilderness

New France's governor, Daniel de Rémy, Sieur de Courcelles, wanted to increase New France's boundaries. So, he quickly granted La Salle permission to explore the Ohio River and its surrounding area. Soon after receiving Courcelles's consent, La Salle sold his land to fund the voyage.

La Salle's expedition left Montreal on July 6, 1669. La Salle and his men traveled down the St. Lawrence River with a group of **missionaries**. Twenty-seven days later, the men reached Lake Ontario. Continuing south, they entered Irondequoit Bay. There, La Salle spent time with the natives of the area.

Then, the party decided to split. The **Sulpician** missionaries turned to the north to reach more native tribes. La Salle continued south. He wasn't done searching for North America's great waterway.

In late autumn 1669, La Salle reached the Ohio River. He sailed down it as far as present-day Louisville, Kentucky.

1618		1637		1645
Raleigh died		Jacques Marquette born		Louis Jolliet born
	1631		1643	
	Smith died		René-Robert Cavelier de La Salle born	

There, he encountered strong **rapids**. La Salle then realized that this was not the passage to the sea.

Still, he wanted to continue on. The other explorers did not. One night, all but one man abandoned La Salle. Despite this loss, La Salle did not feel defeated. In autumn 1670, he returned to Montreal with large bundles of furs.

When La Salle lived in Montreal, only a few hundred people called the area home. Today, Montreal has a population of more than 1 million people!

A New Empire

La Salle dreamed of a vast French empire in the New World. He wanted to find a route that would allow for commercial voyages from the Great Lakes to the Mississippi River. This was a huge project. He knew he needed support.

In 1672, a new governor arrived in New France. Luckily for La Salle, Governor Louis de Buade shared his vision. Buade also wanted to establish a French empire in the New World. The two men spent many nights making plans.

La Salle was not the only explorer interested in the Mississippi River. In 1673, Jacques Marquette and Louis Jolliet returned from their exploration of the mysterious Mississippi. They did not travel the entire river. But, they determined that the Mississippi led to the Gulf of Mexico.

La Salle traveled to France in 1674 and 1677. On his first visit, he obtained ownership of Fort Frontenac on Lake Ontario. At that time, King Louis XIV also awarded La Salle

1669
La Salle explored Ohio region

1666
La Salle sailed to Canada

1673
Marquette and Jolliet explored the Mississippi River

the rank of nobility. He then became known as Sieur de La Salle. And, he received trade rights in New France.

On La Salle's second visit to France, the king granted him permission to explore western New France. However, La Salle would have to pay for his own expeditions. Henry de Tonti accompanied La Salle back to New France. Tonti soon became La Salle's most trusted friend.

After hearing Marquette and Jolliet's findings, La Salle became more determined to explore the length of the Mississippi.

The Great Lakes

In August 1679, La Salle began his next exploration from Fort Frontenac. His crew sailed aboard the *Griffon*, which was about 55 feet (17 m) long. It had been made to withstand the rough waters of the Great Lakes and to carry many furs.

La Salle made his way through Lakes Ontario, Erie, Huron, and Michigan. At present-day Green Bay, Wisconsin, his men loaded the *Griffon* with furs. La Salle sent the ship back to the Niagara River. There, the crew was to transport the furs to another boat. Then, the *Griffon* was to return with supplies.

Meanwhile, La Salle and his group of 14 men continued by canoe to Lake Michigan's southeast shore. There, they built Fort Miami at present-day St. Joseph, Michigan.

In December 1679, La Salle's group left the fort to search for the Mississippi. They canoed down the St. Joseph River. Then, they **portaged** their canoes to the Kankakee River.

1675
Marquette died

1682
La Salle's second Mississippi River expedition

1679
La Salle's first Mississippi River expedition

When the *Griffon* sailed away, La Salle was left with 4 canoes and just 14 men.

Continuing on, La Salle's group reached the Illinois River. They built Fort Crèvecoeur, near today's Peoria, Illinois. There, they waited for their supplies. In 1680, La Salle gave up the wait for the *Griffon*. He headed back to New France on foot. La Salle told Tonti to stay behind and watch over the fort. The *Griffon* never returned. Its fate is unknown.

1687
La Salle died

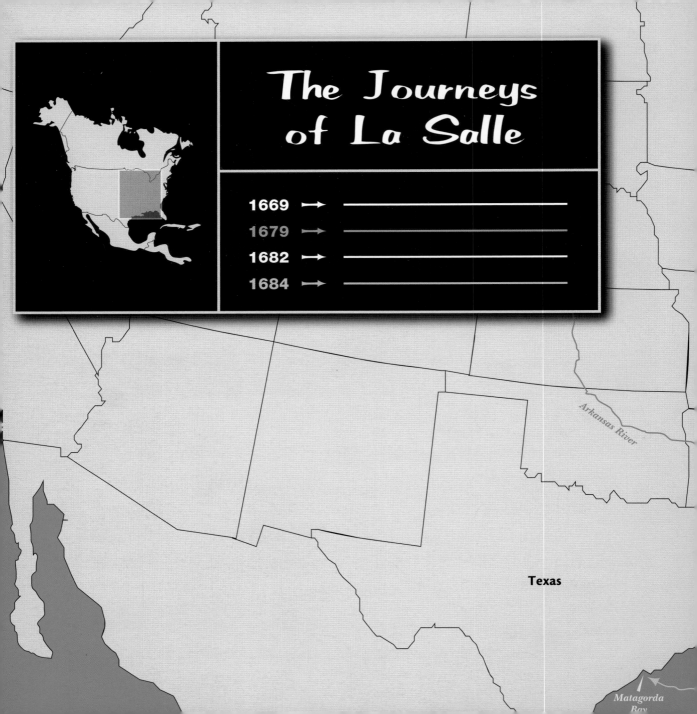

The Journeys of La Salle

1669 →
1679 →
1682 →
1684 →

Arkansas River

Texas

Matagorda Bay

The Great River

La Salle returned to Fort Crèvecoeur with supplies. He found the fort abandoned. Instead of dwelling on this misfortune, La Salle pushed on. La Salle, Tonti, and the other survivors eventually met up in June 1681. Now La Salle could set out on his second exploration of the Mississippi.

The expedition entered the Mississippi on February 6, 1682. On March 13, the group came upon the mouth of the Arkansas River. This was the most southern point that Marquette and Jolliet had reached in 1673.

On April 9, 1682, La Salle's group reached the Gulf of Mexico. There, La Salle held a solemn ceremony. He claimed the entire Mississippi River **basin** for France. He named the region Louisiana, after King Louis.

La Salle had accomplished his goal. Now, he needed to get back to Quebec to spread the news! However, this time the expedition had to travel upstream. This proved much more difficult.

1770
William Clark born

1786
Sacagawea born

1774
Meriwether Lewis born

1800
Sacagawea captured

La Salle and his men did not like the area at the mouth of the Mississippi. The ground was so wet that they could not build a fire. They started their journey back to Quebec on April 10, 1682.

Trying Times

On the return journey, La Salle became ill. He finally recovered enough to travel slowly. However, the bad luck continued. La Salle learned that New France's most recent governor was a rival. Governor Lefèvre de La Barre was not interested in a French empire in the New World. He took control of Fort Frontenac away from La Salle.

In 1683, La Salle established Fort St. Louis at Starved Rock on the Illinois River. But, La Barre seized Fort St. Louis as well. La Salle felt he had only one option left. He sailed back to France to make his appeal to King Louis. The king returned Fort Frontenac and Fort St. Louis to La Salle. Last, King Louis agreed to a new expedition.

La Salle began voyage preparations. This time, he would enter the mouth of the Mississippi by way of the Gulf of Mexico. King Louis supplied four ships filled with settlers for France's new territory!

1804
Lewis and Clark began exploring the Pacific Northwest

1806
Lewis and Clark returned to Missouri

1805
Sacagawea joined the Lewis and Clark expedition

Would You?

Would you be brave enough to approach a king or another ruler with a problem? Do you think La Salle was nervous to speak to King Louis?

Louis XIV became king when he was just four years old! He ruled France for 72 years.

Last Adventure

In 1684, La Salle's **fleet** set sail from France. From the start, this expedition faced many hardships. La Salle and the naval commander quarreled constantly. But that wasn't all. The crew endured shipwrecks and attacks from pirates. Then in the West Indies, La Salle fell ill.

La Salle was not one to give up, so he pushed on. The fleet reached the Gulf of Mexico. But, the men unknowingly sailed past the mouth of the Mississippi! They finally found themselves in today's Matagorda Bay in Texas. La Salle had sailed 500 miles (800 km) west of the Mississippi.

La Salle and the settlers went ashore. They did their best to build a fort and survive. In 1687, La Salle and a small party set out on foot for New France. During their trip, some of La Salle's own men **ambushed** him. The courageous explorer was killed on March 19, 1687.

1809	1812	1838	1856	1881
Lewis died	Sacagawea died	Clark died	Robert Edwin Peary born	Peary entered the U.S. Navy

La Salle's ships landing at Matagorda Bay

René-Robert Cavelier de La Salle was a man with big dreams. Amazingly, he acted on all of them! He was the first European to explore the length of the Mississippi River. And, he established the land empire of Louisiana for his country.

1893
Peary's first expedition

1909
Peary's third expedition, reached the North Pole

1905
Peary's second expedition

1920
Peary died

Glossary

ambush - a surprise attack from a hidden position.

astronomy - the study of objects and matter outside the earth's atmosphere and of their physical and chemical properties.

basin - the entire region of land drained by a river and its tributaries.

dialect - a form of a language spoken in a certain area or by certain people.

Far East - usually considered to consist of the Asian countries bordering on the Pacific Ocean.

fleet - a group of ships under one command.

Jesuit - a member of the Roman Catholic Society of Jesus, which was founded by Saint Ignatius Loyola in 1534.

Louisiana Purchase - land the United States purchased from France in 1803. It extended from the Mississippi River to the Rocky Mountains and from Canada to the Gulf of Mexico.

missionary - a person who spreads a church's religion.

portage - the transporting of boats or goods across land from one body of water to another.

rapid - a fast-moving part of a river. Rocks or logs often break the surface of the water in this area.

strict - severely conforming to a principle or a condition.

Sulpician - a member of the Society of Priests of St. Sulpice, which was founded by Jean Jacques Olier in Paris, France, in 1642.

tutor - to teach a student privately. The teacher is also called a tutor.

Saying It

Crèvecoeur - kreev-KOOR
Frontenac - frawnt-NAWK
Henry de Tonti - ahn-ree duh tohn-tee
Irondequoit Bay - ihr-AHN-duh-kwoyt BAY
Kankakee - kang-kuh-KEE
La Flèche - luh FLEHSH
Louis de Buade - lwee duh byoo-awd
Rouen - ru-AHN
Seine - SEHN
Sulpician - suhl-PIH-shuhn

Web Sites

To learn more about La Salle, visit ABDO Publishing Company on the World Wide Web at **www.abdopublishing.com**. Web sites about La Salle are featured on our Book Links page. These links are routinely monitored and updated to provide the most current information available.

Marco Polo   *Sir Walter Raleigh*   *John Smith*

Robert Peary   *Juan Ponce de León*   *Sacagawea*

Index